I want to be a Musician

Other titles in this series:

I want to be a Builder
I want to be a Cowboy
I want to be a Doctor
I want to be a Firefighter
I want to be a Librarian
I want to be a Mechanic
I want to be a Nurse
I want to be a Pilot
I want to be a Police Officer
I want to be a Teacher
I want to be a Truck Driver
I want to be a Vet
I want to be a Zookeeper

I WANT TO BE A

Musician

DAN LIEBMAN

FIREFLY BOOKS

A FIREFLY BOOK

Published by Firefly Books Ltd. 2003

First Printing

**Publisher Cataloging-in-Publication Data (U.S.)
(Library of Congress Standards)**

Liebman, Dan.
   I want to be a musician / Dan Liebman. —1st ed.
[24] p. : col. photos. ; cm. (I want to be)
Summary: Photographs and easy-to-read text describe the job of a musician.
ISBN 1-55297-760-9
ISBN 1-55297-759-5 (pbk.)
1. Music trade – Vocational guidance – Juvenile literature.
(1. Musicians. 2. Occupations.) I. Title. II. Series.
780/.23 21 ML3795.L54 2003

**National Library of Canada Cataloguing in
Publication Data**

Liebman, Daniel
   I want to be a musician / Dan Liebman.
ISBN 1-55297-760-9 (bound)
ISBN 1-55297-759-5 (pbk.)

1. Musicians – Juvenile literature. I. Title.

ML3795.L716 2003 j780.92   C2003-902826-7

Published in the United States in 2003 by
Firefly Books (U.S.) Inc.
P.O. Box 1338, Ellicott Station
Buffalo, New York, USA., 14205

Published in Canada in 2003 by
Firefly Books Ltd.
3680 Victoria Park Avenue
Toronto, Ontario, Canada, M2H 3K1

Photo Credits

© MediaFocus International, LLC, pages 9, 12,
   front cover & back cover
© Royalty-Free/CORBIS/MAGMA, page 5
© Craig A. Cowan/TSO, pages 7, 15
© Laura Zito, pages 8, 20
© Mark Dixon/Bongo Photo, page 14
© Al Harvey/Slide Farm, pages 21, 23
© George Walker/Firefly Books, pages 6, 9,
   10–11, 13, 16, 17, 18–19, 22, 24

The author and publisher would like to thank:

The A Cups/Toronto
Dr. Christine Choi
Jordan Derouard
Tyler Mahara
Liz Parker/Toronto Symphony Orchestra
Justice C. Prince and Destiny C. Richards
Bryan and Scarlett Scanga
Nicholas Stirling, LuxuriaMusic
Simon Ware

Design by Interrobang Graphic Design Inc.
Printed and bound in Canada by Friesens, Altona, Manitoba

*The Publisher acknowledges the financial support of the Government of Canada through
the Book Publishing Industry Development Program for its publishing activities.*

There are different kinds of music, and there are different jobs that musicians do.

Musicians often play in a group. These musicians are members of a rock band.

Some musicians play classical music. The conductor is leading them.

Some music is written for dancers. All dancers need music when they perform.

Musicians work as teachers, too. They teach you how to play an instrument. They also help you enjoy music.

Playing music can be fun.

Young musicians often start by playing in a student band.

This violinist arrives early at the concert hall.

She is studying the music that she will play tonight.

Musicians write music for television and the movies.

Musicians sometimes travel to different places. Some musicians work outdoors.

This piano teacher also plays in the symphony.

Musicians play at weddings and other parties.